MANNERS MATTER
IN THE
LIBRARY

BY LORI MORTENSEN

ILLUSTRATED BY LISA HUNT

Consultant: Diane R. Chen, Library Information Specialist
John F. Kennedy Middle School, Nashville, Tennessee

CAPSTONE PRESS
a capstone imprint

First Graphics are published by Capstone Press,
151 Good Counsel Drive, P.O. Box 669, Mankato, Minnesota 56002.
www.capstonepub.com

Books published by Capstone Press are manufactured with paper
containing at least 10 percent post-consumer waste.

Library of Congress Cataloging-in-Publication Data
Mortensen, Lori, 1955–
 Manners matter in the library / by Lori Mortensen ; illustrated by Lisa Hunt.
  p. cm. — (First graphics. Manners matter)
 Includes bibliographical references and index.
 ISBN 978-1-4296-5330-5 (library binding)
 ISBN 978-1-4296-6224-6 (paperback)
 1. Library etiquette—Juvenile literature. 2. Library etiquette—Comic books, strips, etc.
3. Graphic novels. I. Hunt, Lisa (Lisa Jane), 1973- ill. II. Title. III. Series.
 Z716.43.M67 2011
 395.5'3—dc22
 [E]   2010026606

Editor: **Shelly Lyons**
Designer: **Juliette Peters**
Art Director: **Nathan Gassman**
Production Specialist: **Eric Manske**

Printed in the United States of America in
Stevens Point, Wisconsin.
092010   005934WZS11

TABLE OF CONTENTS

DO YOU MIND?

We take something with us everywhere we go. Sure, we take things like clothes and cell phones. But we take something else too.

Manners. Manners are the way people treat everyone and everything around them.

Thanks!

When we use good manners, we respect others.

4

It's easy to use good manners. Do you know how to use good manners in the library?

5

Colin and his dad use manners when they get to the library.

Colin's dad uses bad manners when he chats loudly on the phone. He ignores the sign.

Quiet

Colin uses good manners when he tells his dad to turn off the phone.

Thanks, Colin.

CLICK!

Quiet

READ ALL ABOUT IT

There are rows and rows of books and computers at the library. The computer catalog helps Shane and Reese find things.

Sometimes the computers are like carnival rides. The lines can be really long.

When Reese uses bad manners, she sits at the computer forever.

I hope it's my turn soon.

Reese uses good manners when she lets someone else have a turn.

Sorry. I didn't mean to take so long.

There are lots of magazines to read at the library too.

But how many should Ella take at a time? One? Two? Three? A dozen?

Ella grabs a bunch of them. She is using bad manners. Why? Others want to read the magazines too.

Ella uses good manners when she shares the magazines with others. She takes only one or two.

Sam likes to drink and eat while he reads. But that's not a good idea. Reading and eating go together like fish and ice cream!

YUK!

Sam uses bad manners when he spills juice on a book. Food stains stay on the pages forever!

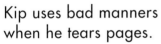

Kip uses bad manners when he tears pages.

riiip!!

When Kip uses good manners, he treats books like new puppies. He turns pages gently.

Library books belong in a certain place. Karl uses bad manners and puts books in any old spot.

Planets

Lions

The *Lions* book should be here.

?

Animals

So where is the right place? Karl uses good manners and follows the librarian's rules. Then librarians put the books in the right spot.

Lions

Animals

RULES, PLEASE

More than anything, people should follow the librarian's rules. Devon, Jim, and Lila use bad manners when they laugh and goof around.

They aren't respecting others in the library.

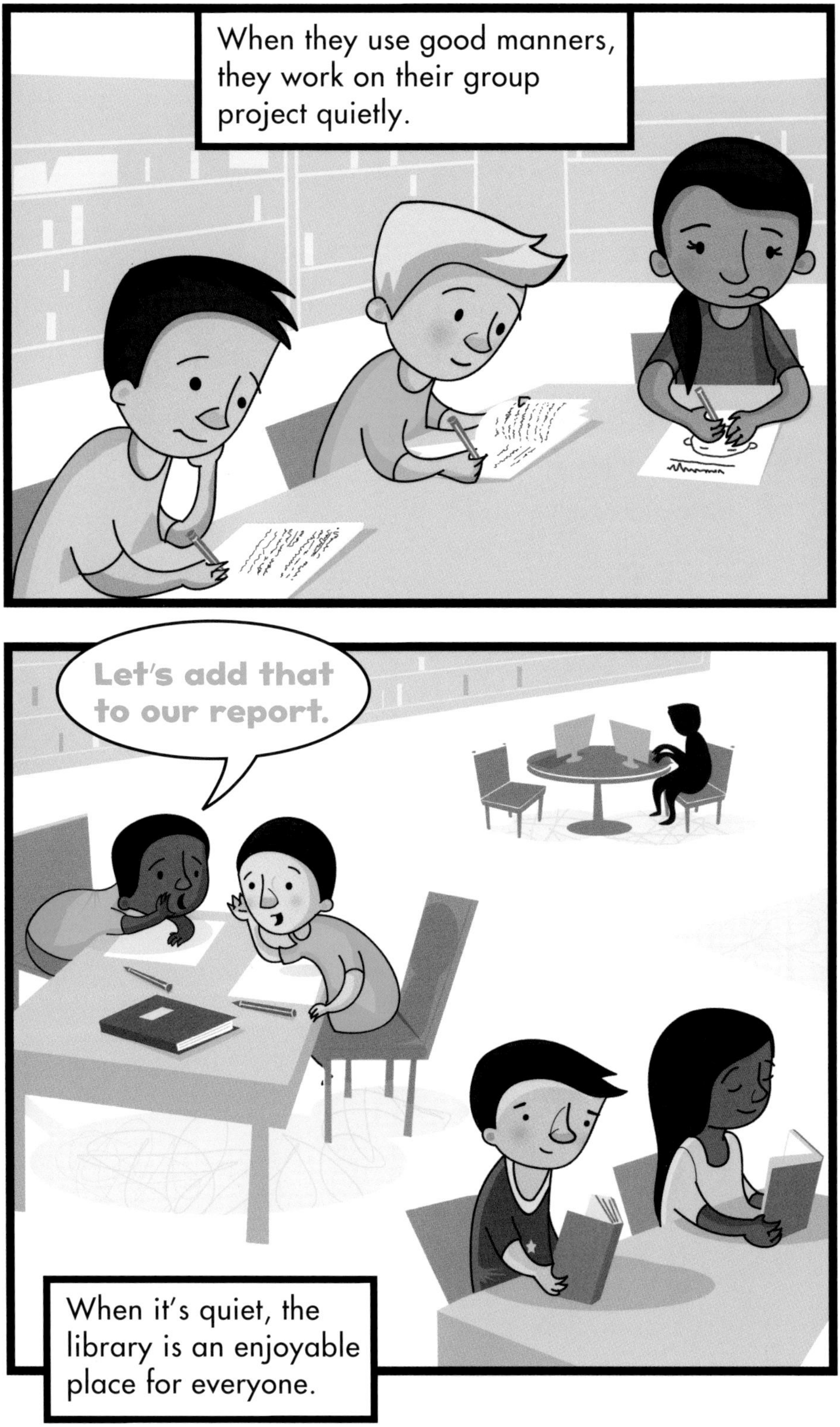
When they use good manners, they work on their group project quietly.
Let's add that to our report.
When it's quiet, the library is an enjoyable place for everyone.

Manners pop up at storytime too. It's easy to spot children using bad manners.

Would everyone please sit in a circle?

Travis, Finn, and Sasha fidget and fuss. They act as if the librarian is not saying anything.

16

When they use good manners, they sit down and listen.

The sooner everyone listens, the more enjoyable storytime will be.

CHECK IT OUT

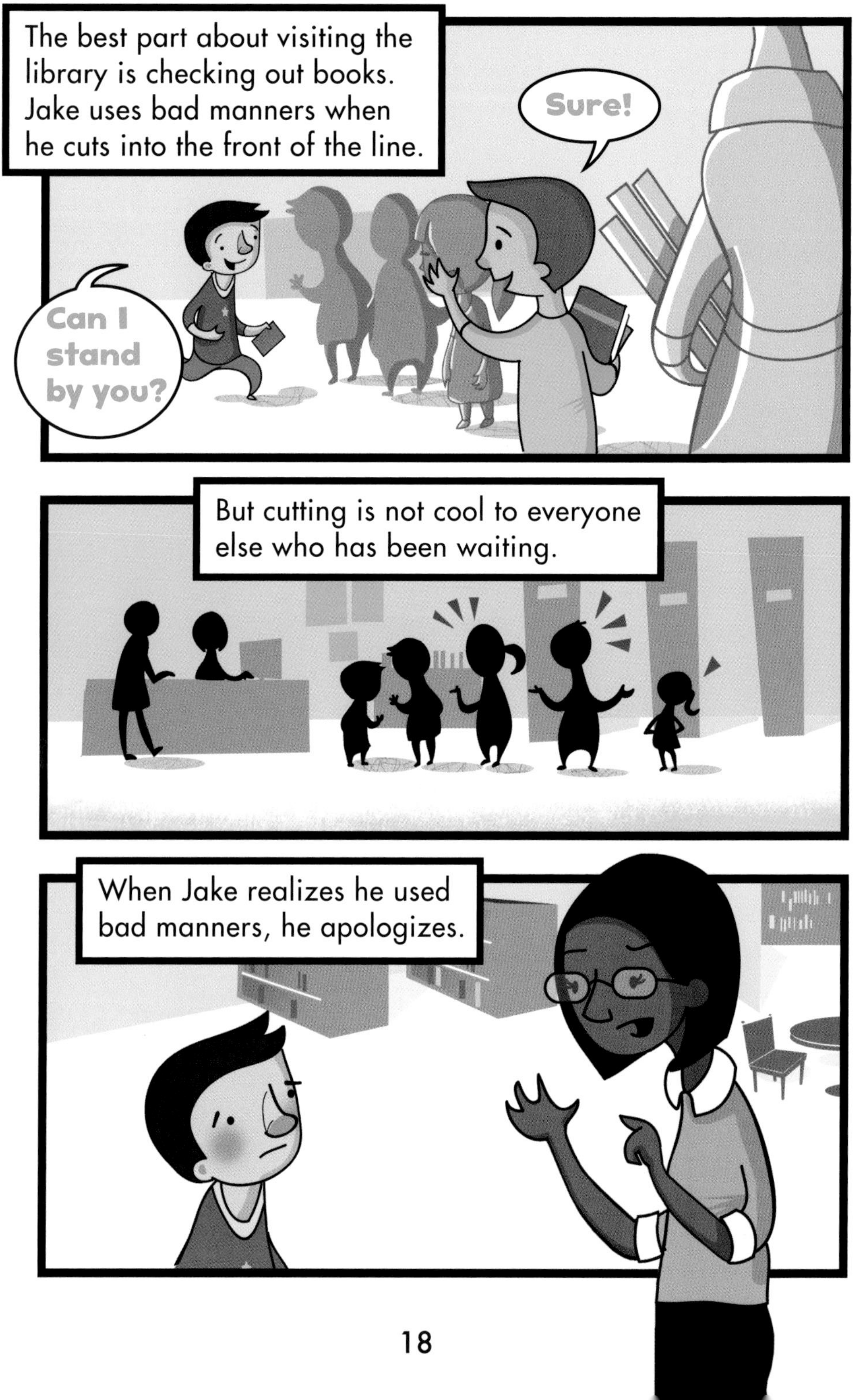
The best part about visiting the library is checking out books. Jake uses bad manners when he cuts into the front of the line.
Can I stand by you?
Sure!
But cutting is not cool to everyone else who has been waiting.
When Jake realizes he used bad manners, he apologizes.

Everyone needs to say "sorry" sometimes.

Oh, sorry.

Thank you.

Chris uses good manners when he waits his turn. He has his library card ready.

Of course, people can't keep library books forever. When books are due, Sarah places them in the book return.

RETURNS

Librarians know whether people used bad manners or good manners.

Oh, dear!

Sarah used bad manners when she folded corners and crinkled pages.

Books treated with good manners last a long time. Lots of people can read them.

People who use good manners are always welcome at the library.

GLOSSARY

apologize—to say you're sorry

book return—a place where people return their books to the library

catalog—a computer in the library where people can look up what books and other materials are available at the library

librarian—someone who works in a library; librarians organize books and other materials

respect—to show you care; respect means to treat others the way you would like to be treated

READ MORE

Finn, Carrie. *Manners in the Library.* Way to Be! Minneapolis: Picture Window Books, 2007.

Keller, Laurie. *Do Unto Otters: A Book about Manners.* New York: Henry Holt, 2007.

Sierra, Judy. *Mind Your Manners, B. B. Wolf.* New York: Knopf, 2007.

Tourville, Amanda Doering. *Manners with a Library Book.* Way to Be! Minneapolis: Picture Window Books, 2009.

INTERNET SITES

FactHound offers a safe, fun way to find Internet sites related to this book. All of the sites on FactHound have been researched by our staff.

Here's all you do:

Visit *www.facthound.com*

Type in this code: 9781429653305

INDEX

Manners Matter

TITLES IN THIS SET: